Berlitz

Learn Spanish with

SUPERMAN™

The Never-Ending Battle

Written by:
Mark Millar

Illustrated by:
Aluir Amancio
Terry Austin
Mike Manley

Colored by:
Marie Severin

Lettered by:
Lois Buhalis

Superman created by **Jerry Siegel** and **Joe Shuster**

Contacting the Editors:
Every effort has been made to provide accurate
information in this publication, but changes are
inevitable. The publisher cannot be responsible
for any resulting loss, inconvenience or injury.
We would appreciate it if readers would call
our attention to any errors or outdated information.

Please contact us at:
Berlitz Publishing
193 Morris Avenue
Springfield, NJ 07081, USA.
E-mail: comments@berlitzbooks.com

Learn Spanish with Superman Volume 2 © 2008 Berlitz Publishing/APA Publications GmbH & Co.
Verlag KG, Singapore Branch, Singapore. All Rights Reserved.

Publishing Director: Sheryl Olinsky Borg
Editor/Project Manager: Emily Bernath
Senior Editor: Lorraine Sova
Editorial Assistant: Eric Zuarino
Interior Design: Claudia Petrilli, Doug Wolff
Production Manager: Elizabeth Gaynor
Cover Design: DC Comics & Claudia Petrilli

hasta la medianoche
until midnight

¿Qué vas a hacer?
What are you going
to do?

3

debe venir a casa
you need to come
home

ahora mismo
right now

medianoche
midnight

¿Y Robin o Batgirl?
And Robin or Batgirl?

muy preocupados
very concerned

sabes
you know

al fin y al cabo
after all

en su lugar
instead

tampoco
either

más importante
more important

¡Dime que no!
Say it ain't so!

tal vez
maybe

o tal vez
or maybe

definitivamente no
absolutely not

vendrá
he'll come

¿Te importa?
Do you mind?

DIOS SANTO, CLARO QUE NO. IT'S A PLEASURE TO FINALLY MEET YOU, SUPERMAN. I'VE BEEN FOLLOWING YOUR CAREER SINCE YOU FIRST APPEARED. BATMAN HOLDS YOU IN THE HIGHEST REGARD.

DE HECHO, I WONDERED IF YOU KNEW POR QUÉ THE HATTER NEVER SAID WHERE HE WAS IF HE'S SO DESPERATE FOR BATMAN TO FIND HIM.

THE CLOCK'S TICKIN' COMMISH.

PORQUE HE FIGURES ONLY BATS HAS WHAT IT TAKES TO HUNT HIM DOWN WITH ZERO CLUES. MUY LISTO, ¿NO?

YOU'RE DEALING WITH A DIFFERENT TYPE OF CRIMINAL NOW, SUPERMAN. GOTHAM CITY NO ES METROPOLIS.

PEOPLE HERE ARE TOO SCARED TO LOOK UP IN THE SKIES...

...Y CRÉEME, THEY HAVE...

UH, COMMISH...? SE HA IDO.

SIGH.

WHAT IS IT WITH THESE PEOPLE?

Dios Santo, claro que no.
Good lord, of course not.

de hecho
actually

por qué
why

porque
because

Muy listo, ¿no?
Pretty smart, huh?

no es
is not

y créeme
and believe me

se ha ido
he's gone

7

no sabe
he doesn't know

cuántos
how many

no sé
I don't know

me siento insultado
I'm insulted

¿Qué tal tú?
How about you?

¡Yo no sé nada!
I don't know anything!

cariño
baby

felicidades
congratulations

¿Perdón?
Excuse me?

ella y sus amigos
she and her friends

mis amigos
my friends

ha fallado
he missed

no es nada personal
it's nothing personal

ahora, si nos
disculpas
now if you'll excuse
us

encantado de
conocerte
nice to meet you

supongo que
I guess that

pero
but

machote
buster

yo puedo
I can

12

buenas noches
good evening

en un minuto
in one minute

¿Qué quieres?
What do you want?

No tenemos
mucho tiempo.
We don't have
much time.

lo juro
I swear

un café
a coffee

ocho minutos
eight minutes

esto no tiene
sentido
this doesn't make
sense

¡Cielo santo!
Good grief!

14

ha hecho trampa
has cheated

por lo tanto
therefore

Prepárense,
chicos y chicas.
Get ready,
boys and girls.

dos minutos
two minutes

¡Escúchame!
Listen to me!

lo siento
I'm sorry

hablo en serio
I'm serious

querida
my dear

pobre
poor

estos sombreros
these hats

¡Tienes que
escucharme!
You have to listen
to me!

un tipo
one guy

ahora
now

AHORA PULL UP, BEFORE IT'S TOO LATE!

¡VALE, VALE!

ALL RIGHT SUPERMAN!

YOU SHOWED THE MAD HATTER WHO ROCKS IN GOTHAM CITY!

OYE, ¿QUÉ PASA? LAST THING I REMEMBER WAS BEING CLOBBERED BY THE MAD HATTER. DOES BATMAN KNOW I'M FLYING HIS BAT-WING?

NO HAY TIEMPO FOR THE DETAILS, SON...

WAY TO GO!

ahora
now

¡Vale, vale!
Okay, okay!

Oye, ¿qué pasa?
Hey, what's
happening?

no hay tiempo
no time

lo único que quería
all I wanted

bueno
well

no puedo
I can't

Oh, iolvídalo!
Oh, never mind!

uno
one

dos
two

el sombrero
the hat

tres
three

¿Está bien?
Are you okay?

¡Oh, no, no te vas!
Oh, no, you don't!

nadie
nobody

ups
oops

¿Ha habido suerte?
Any luck?

horas
hours

qué listo
pretty smart

y aquí está
and here it is

no me imagino
I can't imagine

no hay nada
there's nothing

en serio
really

oh, gracias
oh, thank you

sin duda
no doubt about it

interesante
interesting

gracias
thanks

¿Qué quieres decir?
What's your point?

al contrario
on the contrary

creo que
I think that

de vez en cuando
every once in a while

noventa días
ninety days

¿Qué voy a hacer?
**What am I going
to do?**

¡Sé realista, cariño! OUR DIMENSIONS ONLY CONVERGE EVERY THREE MONTHS. IF I DON'T STRIKE AHORA, IT'S GONNA BE ANOTHER NINETY DAYS BEFORE I CAN TAKE A POP AT THAT BIG, BLUE DOPE.

THIS WOULDN'T BE THE SAME DOPE WHO OUTSMARTS YOU EVERY TIME YOU SHOW YOUR FACE IN LA TERCERA DIMENSION, MR. MXYZPTLK?

SNEAKY DON'T MAKE HIM SMART, MISS GSPTLNZ.

FIVE-DIMENSIONAL IMPS GET A FREE PASS IN THE CUARTA DIMENSIÓN, ¿NO? I CAN JUMP BACK IN TIME AND PICK A FIGHT WITH THE BLUE BOY BEFORE WE EVEN MET!

ADEMÁS, HE'S READY FOR ME NOW WHEN I SLUM IT IN 3-D. THE ELEMENT OF SORPRESA AIN'T ON MY SIDE SINCE HE STARTED MARKIN' OFF MY ARRIVAL DATES ON HIS CALENDAR.

HEY, WAIT A SEC! ¿QUÉ ESTOY PENSANDO?

OUTWITTING AN INEXPERIENCED TEEN OF STEEL SHOULD BE A BREEZE FOR A GUY WITH MY BIG BRAINS! ¡ES UN PLAN PERFECTO!

BRIGHT IDEAS!

HERE WE GO AGAIN...

NOW ALL I HAVE TO DO IS PICK UN DÍA WHEN POOR SUPES WAS AT IS MOST VULNERABLE...

¡Sé realista, cariño!
Get real, sweetie!

ahora
now

la tercera
the third

además
besides

sorpresa
surprise

¿Qué estoy pensando?
What am I thinking?

cuarta dimensión
fourth dimension

¿no?
right?

¡Es un plan perfecto!
It's a perfect plan!

un día
a day

SMALLVILLE, U.S.A. HACE TRECE AÑOS:

CLARK?

CLARK KENT, WHAT'S SO FASCINATING ABOUT A DAMP SPOT ON THE WALL?

HM?

LO SIENTO. I WAS IN A WORLD OF MY OWN.

YOU'RE GOING TO HAVE TO WORK ON THAT CONCENTRATION IF YOU WANT TO BE A JOURNALIST WHEN YOU GRADUATE, YOUNG MAN.

FELICIDADES. YOUR CAREER PAPER CAME TOP OF THE CLASS.

I CAN ONLY HOPE YOUR FASHION SKILLS ARE BETTER THAN YOUR SPELLING, MISS LANG. ANOTHER "F" FOR YOUR COLLECTION.

MEJOR QUE UNA "G," ¿NO?

THEY DON'T DO "G"S, LANA.

hace trece años
thirteen years ago

lo siento
sorry

felicidades
congratulations

Mejor que una "G," ¿no?
Better than a "G," right?

¡Mira!
Look!

¡Es un pájaro!
It's a bird!

¡Es un avión!
It's a plane!

te lo advierto
I'm warning you

Ah ¿sí?
Oh yeah?

vamos
come on

¡Ostras!
Holy cow!

o no
or not

a veces
sometimes

¿Qué tal?
How are you doing?

hijo
son

30

papà
dad

porque
because

antes o después
sooner or later

mis poderes
my powers

hijo
son

un chico
a boy

un hombre
a man

Él no entiende.
He doesn't
understand.

algo
something

claro
sure

¿verdad?
right?

mis padres
my parents

al principio
at first

pero ahora
but now

sí
yes

lo que quería
what I wanted

¡Es perfecto!
It's perfect!

¿Quién eres?
Who are you?

sígueme
follow me

al cabo de un tiempo
after a while

por supuesto
of course

como
like

pero
but

THE EMBARRASSING CLARK KENT ACT WAS DROPPED LIKE A ROCK AND YOU DID WHAT ANY OTHER SUPER-BE-ING WOULD DO ON A PLANET FULL OF LAME-BRAINS ALWAYS MAKIN' MISTAKES...

... YOU TOOK OVER THE WORLD.

THE REST OF THE WORLD WAS FORCED TO LIVE IN THE TOTALITARIAN NIGHTMARE YOUR ADOPTIVE **PADRES** HAD FEARED SINCE THEY FOUND A CERTAIN ROCKET LYING IN A CERTAIN DITCH...

...LANA LANG **SE CASÓ CONTIGO**--A MONSTER SHE COULD NEVER LOVE...

padres
parents

se casó contigo
married you

35

y
and

un niño normal
a normal kid

¡Tienes que creerme!
You've got to believe
me!

claro
sure

sólo
only

pero es tu decisión
but it's your decision

donde
where

una pregunta
a question

en la luna
on the moon

vamos ahora
let's go now

mamá y papá
mom and dad

adios
goodbye

tal vez
maybe

la luna
the moon

bueno
well

chaval
kid

el nombre
the name

el mayor héroe
the greatest hero

¡Chao!
See ya!

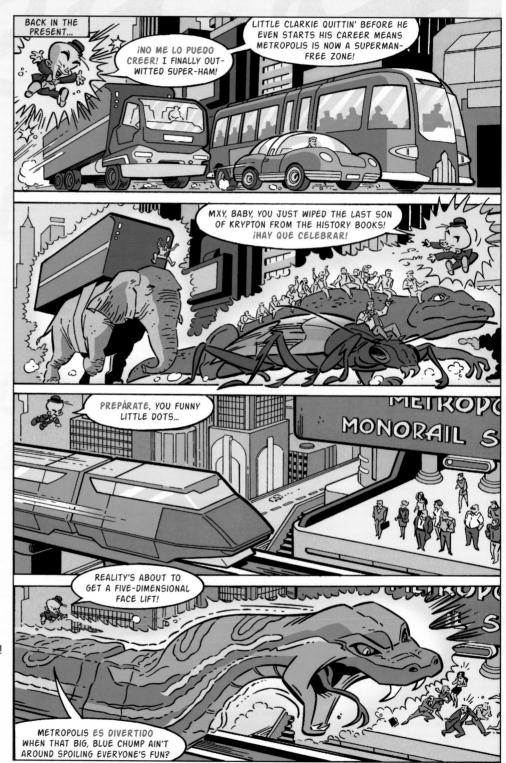

¡No me lo puedo creer!
I don't believe it!

¡Hay que celebrar!
It's celebration time!

prepárate
get ready

es divertido
is fun

40

normalmente
normally

pero esos días
but those days

los juguetes
the toys

necesitamos ayuda
we need help

quítate del medio
outta the way

¡Venga nenas!
**Come on,
you wimps!**

¡Guau!
Wow!

hombre
man

mamá y papá
mom and dad

la única cosa
the only thing

a lo mejor
maybe

42

en el pasado
in the past

vamos
come on

¿Eh?
Huh?

mentía
I lied

un nuevo plan
a new plan

verás
you see

días
days

pero
but

olvídelo
forget it

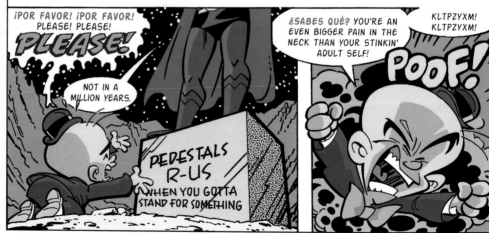

mentí
I lied

¿Cuántas veces...?
How many times...?

Suena bastante
aburrido.
It sounds really
boring.

aburrido
boring

estúpido
dumb

Tengo dieciséis
años.
I'm sixteen
years old.

es penoso
it's pathetic

por favor
please

¿Sabes qué?
You know
something?

quinta
fifth

cuando vuelvas
when you come back

nos vemos
see you around

¿Eh?
Huh?

¡Guau!
Wow!

desayuno
breakfast

la escuela
school

de hecho
actually

papà
dad

¿No?
No?

decisión
decision

hijo
son

veamos
let's see

HOW MUCH CAN ONE MAN HATE?

MARK MILLAR
WRITER
ALUIR AMANCIO
PENCILLER
TERRY AUSTIN
INKER
MARIE SEVERIN
COLORS
ZYLONOL
SEPS
LOIS BUHALIS
LETTERS
FRANK BERRIOS
ASSISTANT
MIKE McAVENNIE
EDITOR

OPEN THE WINDOW, MERCY.

TENEMOS VISITA.

SUPERMAN CREATED BY JERRY SIEGEL & JOE SHUSTER

Tenemos visita.
We've got a visitor.

como siempre
as usual

déjate de juegos
stop playing games

créeme
believe me

si no me crees
if you don't believe me

48

OH, THEY'RE ALL IN PERFECT ORDER, *ESTOY SEGURO.*

¿QUÉ PASA, SUPERMAN? YOU'RE STARTING TO SOUND A LITTLE PARANOID. DON'T TELL ME THE JOB'S STARTING TO GET TO YOU.

STILL, THE NUMBER OF PSYCHOPATHS OUT THERE TRYING TO KILL YOU ON A DAILY BASIS MUST BE RATHER STRESSFUL. *AL FIN Y AL CABO,* THEY ONLY HAVE TO BE LUCKY ONCE, BUT YOU HAVE TO BE LUCKY ALL THE TIME.

¿POR QUÉ LO HACES, LUTHOR? WHY DO YOU WASTE ALL THIS TIME AND ENERGY? IS IT THE POWERS? IS IT THAT I HAVE HAIR?

WHAT HAVE I EVER DONE TO MAKE YOU HATE ME THIS MUCH?

IF YOU HAVE TO ASK, *NUNCA LO SABRÁS.*

MANIAC.

estoy seguro
I'm sure

¿Qué pasa?
What's the matter?

al fin y al cabo
after all

¿Por qué lo haces?
Why do you do it?

nunca lo sabrás
you'll never know

el coche
the car

¿Estás seguro?
Are you sure?

buenas ideas
good ideas

"...BESIDES, WHAT GREATER SOURCE OF INSPIRATION FOR A NEW PLAN THAN WATCHING THEM LINE UP TO TOUCH THE HEM OF HIS CAPE?"

SE HACE TARDE. EVERYONE ELSE LEFT HOURS AGO.

IS THIS STATUE REALLY SUCH A BIG DEAL? *QUIERO DECIR,* HOW MANY SCHOOLS AND HOSPITALS HAVE YOUR NAME ABOVE THE DOORWAY, HUH?

ALL PAID FOR WITH MY OWN *DINERO,* MERCY.

THIS NEVER COST SUPERMAN A PENNY.

A NEW PLAN BEGINNING TO FORM?

¿QUÉ TE PARECE, MY DEAR?

THIS IS MY MOST PERFECT SCHEME YET.

Se hace tarde.
It's getting late.

quiero decir
I mean

dinero
money

¿Qué te parece?
What do you think?

no me lo
puedo creer
I can't believe it

bueno
well

supongo que
I guess

¿Qué haces?
What are you doing?

¿Dónde ha ido Kent?
Where'd Kent go?

en la estación del
metro
in the subway
station

No por
mucho tiempo.
Not for
much longer.

bastante feo
pretty ugly

TAKE ALL THE PICTURES YOU WANT, BOYS AND GIRLS. JUST BE SURE TO CATCH MY BEST SIDE PARA LAS DAMAS.

BONITO TRABAJO, AMIGO. IT'S ALWAYS NICE TO MEET SOMEONE ELSE IN THE SAME LINE OF WORK. ¿CÓMO TE LLAMAS?

SUPERIOR-MAN, ¡POR SUPUESTO! HOW ELSE DO YOU DESCRIBE THE ONE GUY IN METROPOLIS STRONGER THAN SUPERMAN?

GET USED TO THE NAME, FOLKS. IT'S GOING TO BE EVERYWHERE ONCE I CATCH THE CROOKS THE MAN OF STEEL COULDN'T.

LOIS LANE, DAILY PLANET. ARE YOU SAYING THAT SUPERMAN HAS A PARTNER?

OH, NOT A PARTNER, PRECIOSA...

...A REPLACEMENT.

para las damas
for the ladies

Bonito trabajo, amigo.
Nice job, friend.

¿Cómo te llamas?
What's your name?

por supuesto
of course

preciosa
gorgeous

55

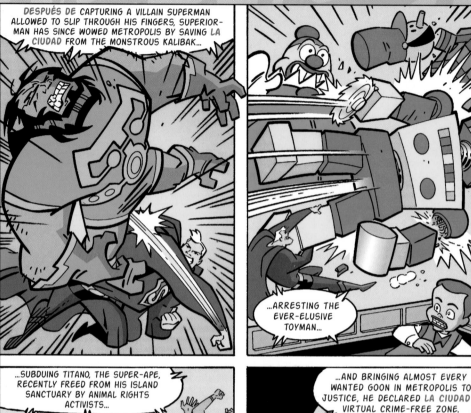

DESPUÉS DE CAPTURING A VILLAIN SUPERMAN ALLOWED TO SLIP THROUGH HIS FINGERS, SUPERIOR-MAN HAS SINCE WOWED METROPOLIS BY SAVING *LA CIUDAD* FROM THE MONSTROUS KALIBAK...

...ARRESTING THE EVER-ELUSIVE TOYMAN...

...SUBDUING TITANO, THE SUPER-APE, RECENTLY FREED FROM HIS ISLAND SANCTUARY BY ANIMAL RIGHTS ACTIVISTS...

...AND BRINGING ALMOST EVERY WANTED GOON IN METROPOLIS TO JUSTICE, HE DECLARED *LA CIUDAD* A VIRTUAL CRIME-FREE ZONE.

IS IT ANY WONDER PEOPLE ARE SUDDENLY ASKING: *NECESITAMOS A SUPERMAN?*

después de
after

la ciudad
the city

¿Necesitamos a Superman?
Do we need Superman?

56

PERO THE MOST DRAMATIC OF ALL IS THE STATEMENT ABOUT TO BE MADE HERE AT THE HEADQUARTERS OF LEXCORP INTERNATIONAL...

DAMAS Y CABALLEROS, LEXCORP IS PROUD TO ANNOUNCE OUR FORMAL PARTNERSHIP WITH SUPERIOR-MAN IN LIGHT OF THE BREATHTAKING CHANGES HE'S MADE TO METROPOLIS IN SUCH A SHORT TIME.

KLIK KLIK! FAASH!

COMBINING OUR TECHNOLOGY WITH HIS STRENGTH AND ENTHUSIASM, WE FIRMLY BELIEVE WE CAN TURN ESTA CIUDAD INTO A UTOPIA.

THE SKY IS NO LONGER THE LIMIT.

FAASH!

KLIK KLIK

FANS OF EL NUEVO HÉROE IN METROPOLIS WERE ECSTATIC.

A PLAIN-SPEAKING ATTITUDE THAT APPEALS TO EVERYONE.

TACKLING PROBLEMS EVEN SUPERMAN DIDN'T TOUCH.

BUT ONE QUESTION STILL REMAINS:

¿QUIÉN ES SUPERIOR-MAN Y ¿DE DÓNDE ES?

pero
but

damas y caballeros
ladies and gentlemen

esta ciudad
this city

el nuevo héroe
the new hero

¿Quién es Superior-man
Who is Superior-man

...y ¿de dónde es?
...and where is he from?

¿Y ahora qué?
What's next?

amigo
friend

ni lo sueñes
dream on

bueno, en ese caso
well, in that case

¿Por qué es siempre
Luthor?
Why is it always
Luthor?

de hecho
actually

el plan de reserva
the backup plan

un secundo
a second

pero tú no
entiendes eso
but you don't
understand that

Sí, es correcto.
Yes, that's right.

¿Dónde estoy?
Where am I?

mi cabeza
my head

cálmate
stay calm

querida mía
my dear

dile que
tell him that

por lo menos
at least

no
no

viejo amigo
old friend

ahora
now

muy muy despacio
very very slowly

¿Pero qué rayos?
What the heck?

dulces sueños
sweet dreams

oh no
oh no

muy listo
very clever

¿Ustedes dos
están bien?
Are you two okay?

control absoluto
absolute control

esta vez
this time

¿Cuántos?
How many?

el mundo
the world

sí
yes

absolutamente nada
absolutely nothing

mi vida
my life

¡Definitivamente no!
Absolutely not!

el año que viene
next year

hace años
years ago

¿Qué haces?
What are you
doing?

míralo
look at it

Magnífico,
¿no es cierto?
Magnificent,
isn't it?

Precisamente, papá.
Precisely, father.

algún día
someday

y todo el mundo
and everyone

¡Es inútil!
It's no use!

bueno
well

!Es una trampa!
It's a trap!

¡AQUÍ ESTÁ! THE TACTICAL GENIUS OF KALIBAK, SON OF DARKSEID AND PRINCE OF APOKOLIPS! WHO ELSE COULD BEST SUPERMAN SO EASILY?

WHO ELSE WOULD DEVISE UNA TRAMPA SO MERCILESSLY CUNNING?

YOU SHOULDN'T BE AQUÍ, KALIBAK! WHAT ABOUT THE AGREEMENT?

APOKOLIPS PROMISED NO MORE PHYSICAL ATTACKS AGAINST EARTH, SUPERMAN, BUT I'VE DEVISED A BITTER GENOCIDE CRAFTED TO LEAVE MY KNUCKLES STAIN-FREE...

YOU AND I ARE SWAPPING BRAINS, GAUDY BUTTERFLY!

DATE PRISA WITH THAT LOCK, JIMMY! WE'RE RUNNING OUT OF TIME

MI PADRE WILL APPRECIATE THIS SURPRISE! YOU TRAPPED FOREVER IN MY TWISTED FORM, WHILE I CRUSH THE EARTH WITH YOUR SUPER-FISTS!

THE MIND-TRADER WILL MAKE THIS DREAM A REALITY, SUPERMAN...

...ALL I HAVE TO DO IS PRESS A BUTTON.

¡ESPERA! JIMMY, NO!

¡Aquí está!
Here it is!

una trampa
a trap

aquí
here

date prisa
hurry up

mi padre
my father

¡Espera!
Wait!

71

¿Eres tú?
Is that you?

idiota
idiot

¡Oh no!
Oh no!

¡Tenemos que hacer algo!
We have to do something!

¡Demasiado tarde!
Too late!

hey
hey

lo siento
sorry

verá
you see

verdad
right

recuerdas
remember

Tienes toda la razón.
You're absolutely
right.

¡Luego nos vemos!
Catch you later!

no te ofendas
no offense

por cierto
by the way

dame un respiro
give me a break

veinte minutos
twenty minutes

vale
okay

¿Y ahora qué?
So what now?

claro
of course

pensé
I thought

pensaste
you thought

perdón
forgive me

una hora y un lugar
a time and a place

pero papá
but father

¡Silencio!
Silence!

como desee
as you wish

otra vez
again

tal vez
perhaps

al fin y al cabo
after all

eso es cierto
this is true

tu amigo
your friend

¡CHÉVERE!

BUENO, JIMMY, ACCORDING TO OUR TESTS, EVERY MOLECULE IN YOUR BODY CHECKS OUT AS ONE HUNDRED PERCENT KRYPTONIAN.

IF YOU DIDN'T SAY "COOL" EVERY TEN SECONDS, I'D SWEAR I WAS ACTUALLY TALKING TO THE MAN OF STEEL HIMSELF.

TESTING JIMMY'S STRENGTH ISN'T GOING TO BRING SUPERMAN BACK, PROFESSOR HAMILTON. WE NEED S.T.A.R. LABS TO LEND US A SPACESHIP SO WE CAN TRAVEL TO APOKOLIPS AND RESCUE HIM.

MI QUERIDA LOIS, APOKOLIPS ISN'T A WORLD SEPARATED FROM US LIKE MARS OR VENUS OR THANAGAR.

APOKOLIPS EXISTS IN A HIGHER DIMENSION WHICH, AS FAR AS I'M AWARE, CAN ONLY BE ACCESSED BY THEIR BOOM TUBES AND OTHER TECHNOLOGY NATIVE TO THEIR CIVILIZA-TION.

I KNOW S.T.A.R. HAS BEEN INVOLVED IN CERTAIN TRANSDIMENSIONAL RESEARCH, BUT IT COULD TAKE FOREVER TO FIND THE RIGHT FREQUENCY.

POR AHORA, I'M AFRAID, SUPERMAN IS TRAPPED ON APOKOLIPS, AND JIMMY MUST CARRY OUT HIS DUTIES.

G-GULP

bueno
well

chévere
cool

mi querida
my dear

por ahora
for now

aguanta
hang in there

apágala
turn it off

sin volverse loco
without going nuts

un sol amarillo
a yellow sun

¡Un segundo!
Wait a sec!

¿El qué?
What?

vamos
come on

¡Mi madre!
Holy geez!

¿Sí?
Yeah?

¿Qué problema
tienes, colega?
What's the
problem, fella?

¿Qué estoy pensando?
What am I thinking?

soy
I'm

qué narices
what the heck

¡Frena!
Hit the brakes!

los ojos cerrados
my eyes closed

bonito trabajo
nice work

eh?
huh?

soy yo
I am

¿Quién?
Who?

es
is

Mala suerte, ¿eh?
Bad luck, huh?

peor aún
worse still

lo siento
I'm sorry

aquí
here

repito
I repeat

nadie
no one

¡Estás solo!
You're on your own!

todavía no
not yet

¡Es imposible!
This is impossible!

Nada es
imposible.
Nothing is
impossible.

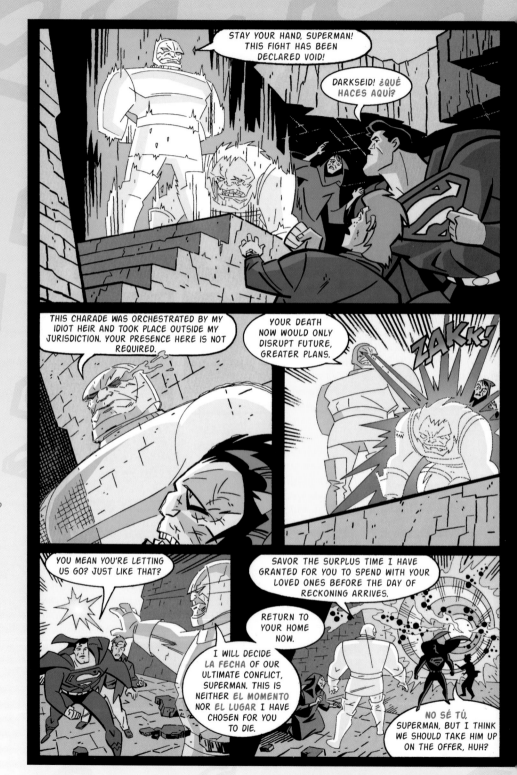

¿Qué haces aquí?
What are you
doing here?

la fecha
the date

el momento
the time

el lugar
the place

No sé tú
I don't know
about you

antes de irte
before you depart

hasta la próxima
until next time

Nos vamos a casa.
We're going home.

un segundo
wait a sec

bueno
well

¿Algún problema?
Is something wrong?

tres refrescos
three sodas

dos hamburguesas
con queso
two cheeseburgers

y papas fritas
and french fries

lo siento
sorry

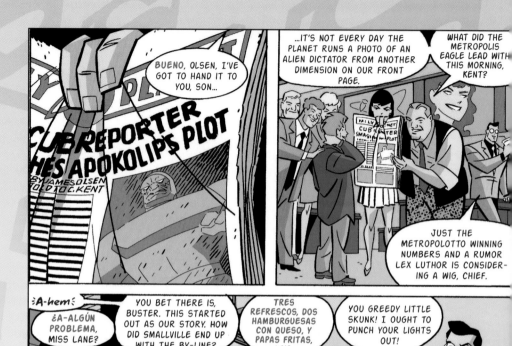

¡Guau!
Wow!

aquí
over here

soy
I am

¿Quién eres tú,
perdedor?
Who are you,
loser?

¿Qué?
What?

precioso
gorgeous

me llamo
my name is

SUPERMAN BRING BIZARRO HERE TO LOOK AFTER KRYPTO. ME HAPPY PROTECTING BIZARRO'S BEST FRIEND. ES UN PERRO EXCELENTE.

WELL, IF YER HAVIN' SUCH A GREAT TIME HERE, WHY YA WANNA HITCH A RIDE BACK TA EARTH, IDI-OTA?

AMO A KRYPTO, SPIKY-HAIR MAN, BUT ME NEED MORE ON BIZARRO WORLD THAN JUST PRETTY FACE AND INTELLIGENT CONVERSATION.

BIZARRO WANT A WIFE, TOO. ME DESPERATE TO SEE LOIS AGAIN.

LOIS...LANE? YA MEAN SUPERGEEK'S MAIN SQUEEZE?

HECK, WHY DIDN'T YA SAY SO BEFORE? CLIMB ABOARD FACE-ACHE!

SPIKY-HAIR MAN TAKE BIZARRO HOME?

MEJOR TODAVÍA, BUB--I'M GONNA PERSONALLY SET YOU GUYS UP AN' MAKE SURE SUPERMAN DON'T GET IN THE WAY, EITHER!

SOB! THIS AM HAPPIEST MOMENT OF BIZARRO'S LIFE!

¡CHAO KRYPTO! ME COME BACK FOR YOU SOON!

MAYBE YOU BE BRIDESMAID IF BIZARRO AND LOIS TIE KNOT, EH?

MAN, THIS IS GONNA BE FRAGGIN' HILARIOUS!

Es un perro excelente.
He's an excellent dog.

idiota
moron

amo a
I love

mejor todavía
better than that

chao
bye

amo a
I love

tiene que ser
that's got to be

¡Eso no es justo!
That's no fair!

vamos
come on

¿Pero qué...?
What the...?

Hey, no me
mires a mí.
Hey, don't
look at me.

¿Dónde está Clark?
Where's Clark?

uy
uh-oh

aléjate de
get away from

no te preocupes
don't worry

¡Por Dios!
Good lord!

perfecto
perfect

ciudad
city

Bueno,
éste es gratis.
Well this one's free.

eres
you are

sí, bueno
yes, well

no me digas
don't tell me

de hecho
in fact

cita
date

estupendo
terrific

pero no tengo dinero
but I don't have any money

es muy amable
that's very thoughtful

¿Quieres probarlos?
You want to try them?

no importa
that's okay

oh Dios mío
oh my God

no entiendo
I don't understand

la cita
the date

¡Llama a la policía!
Call the cops!

tranquilito
calm down

¡NO! ¡MENTIRA!

SKKRRRSH

ELEEEK!

IT NOT MATTER IF ME UGLY! LOIS STILL WANT TO BE BIZARRO'S WIFE!

LO SIENTO, BIZARRO. SÓLO QUIERO SER TU AMIGA.

SIGH. ME HEAR HEARTBEAT JUMP WHEN YOU NOT TELL TRUTH, LOIS.

IT'S NOTHING PERSONAL. HONEST. I THINK YOU'RE A REALLY SWEET GUY, BUT THAT'S ALL I CAN COMMIT TO RIGHT NOW.

THAT AM REASON BIZARRO MUST MAKE US BOTH THE SAME.

SOMOS DIFERENTES. THAT WHY BEAUTIFUL GIRL REPORTER COULD NEVER LOVE FREAKY MONSTER LIKE BIZARRO.

¡No! ¡Mentira!
No! That's a lie!

lo siento
I'm sorry

Sólo quiero ser
tu amiga.
I only want to be
your friend.

somos diferentes
we're different

101

CREO QUE NO. I DON'T THINK "LOIS BIZARRO" HAS A NICE RING TO IT...

¿QUÉ PASA, SUPES? MAD COZ YER BABE DUMPED YA FER A PUNK WITH THE VOCABULARY OF A FOUR-YEAR-OLD?

LOIS DOESN'T BELONG TO ME, OR ANYONE ELSE, MISTER.

THWAK

OOF!

...BUT HERE'S SOMETHING THAT DOES!

ES MI AMIGA. I'M ANGRY BECAUSE SHE'S AT THE MERCY OF A CREATURE INCAPABLE OF REASON. BIZARRO IS LIKE A CHILD, AND IF HIS AFFECTIONS ARE SPURNED, WHO KNOWS WHAT HE'LL DO.

Creo que no.
I don't think so.

¿Qué pasa?
What's the matter?

Es mi amiga.
She's my friend.

THWOKK

POOM!

OH, I KNOW *EXACTAMENTE* WHAT HE'LL DO!

THAT PASTY-FACED DWEEB ALMOST BORED ME TO DEATH ALL THE WAY HERE ABOUT HOW HE'S GONNA TURN THE LANE CHICK INTO A BIZARRO!

¿QUÉ?! THEN I CAN'T WASTE TIME WITH YOU! I'VE GOT TO--

YOU'VE GOT TA JUST SIT HERE TILL I LET YA UP.

NO LLORES, MR. CLEAN-CUT! I'LL LET YA SAVE LANE, PROVIDIN' YA DO SOMETHIN' FER ME. BOY SCOUT LIKE YOU PROBABLY HATES SMOKIN'...

...BUT LIGHT ME UP WITH YER HEAT-VISION AN' THE TWO OF US ARE QUITS.

¿NO LO SABES, LOBO?

exactamente
exactly

¿Qué?!
What?!

no llores
don't cry

¿No lo sabes?
Don't you know?

¡Vale, ya está bien!
Alright, that's it!

vamos
come on

caballeros
gentlemen

¡No seas idiota!
Don't be such an
idiot!

no hay tiempo
there's no time

¡Dale fuerte!
Kick his butt!

...AND IT'S A SAFE BET WHERE BIZARRO'S TAKEN HER.

LEX LUTHOR'S ABANDONED LABORATORY EN LAS MONTAÑAS...

...THE PLACE WHERE BIZARRO HIMSELF WAS CREATED FROM A STOLEN SAMPLE OF MY OWN D.N.A.

HMMM... JUDGING FORM THE WAY THESE MACHINES HAVE BEEN PUT TOGETHER, HE'S DEFINITELY AQUÍ.

BIZARRO? THERE'S NO POINT HIDING IN THE SHADOWS, AMIGO.

I CAN PINPOINT EXACTLY WHERE YOU ARE IN A HUNDRED DIFFERENT WAYS.

POR FAVOR NOT STOP ME CREATING BIZARRO LOIS LANE, SUPERMAN.

ME ONLY WANT SOMEONE TO HOLD AT NIGHT WHEN ME WATCH TWIN SUNS GO DOWN ON BIZARRO WORLD. ME SIENTO SOLO.

I...I KNOW IT MUST BE TOUGH, BIZARRO, BUT DOING THIS WON'T MAKE YOU FEEL BETTER. WE'RE TWO OF A KIND, DEEP DOWN.

YOU DON'T WANT TO HURT LOIS ANY MORE THAN I DO.

LO SIENTO, SUPERMAN. BIZARRO GET CONFUSED...

en las montañas
in the mountains

aquí
here

amigo
friend

por favor
please

Me siento solo.
I'm lonely.

lo siento
sorry

...QUERÍA DECIR--SUPERMAN TOO LATE TO STOP PROCESS!

ME MAKE BIZARRO LOIS HACE DIEZ MINUTOS!

KZIK!

SANTO CIELO...

LOIS!

BIZARRO LOIS AM MANUFACTURED USING STUPID MACHINES LUTHOR DAMAGED DURING EXPLOSION LAST TIME, SUPERMAN.

THAT WHY SHE NOT ABLE TO WALK AND TALK LIKE ME PREFER...

...BUT ME WANT TO MARRY IMPERFECT GIRL REPORTER, ANYWAY.

querÍa decir
I meant to say

hace diez minutos
ten minutes ago

Santo Cielo
good lord

¡Espera!
Wait!

Superman se está
volviendo loco.
Superman is
going crazy.

felicidades
congratulations

relájate
lighten up

¿Por qué?
Why?

ABOUT TIME YOU NOTICED.

ESTÁS... ESTÁS BIEN...!

¡OYE! IF THAT'S THE REAL LANE BABE, WHO'S THE EYESORE?

THAT AM BIZARRO'S FIANCÉE. SHE AM DUPLICATE OF ORIGINAL LOIS, JUST LIKE BIZARRO AM COPY OF SUPER-MAN, ESTÚPIDO!

ME ALWAYS WANTED GIRL WHO COULD KEEP LUNCH DOWN WHEN SHE LOOK AT BIZARRO, AND BIZARRO LOIS HAVE STRONG STOMACH!

US AM PERFECT MATCH!

BLEEEAH!

SPOIL YOUR FUN AND GAMES, LOBO?

FUN? ¿DE QUÉ HABLAS? EARTH'S EVERY BIT AS CRUMMY AN' ROMANTIC AS I REMEMBERED! I'VE GOT A JOB TO DO ON THE OTHER SIDE OF THE UNIVERSE, SUPES...

...AN' IF I EVER SEE SUCH A SORRY COLLECTION OF SOPPY GEEKS AN' DWEEBS AGAIN, IT'LL BE A BILLION AÑOS TOO SOON!

KRAASH

estás bien
you're all right

¡Oye!
Hey!

estúpido
stupid

¿De qué hablas?
What are you talking about?

años
years

te echaba de menos
I missed you

nueva mamá
new mom

tan feliz
so happy